This book belongs to:

____

Made in the USA
Las Vegas, NV
27 August 2021

29074875R00066